a year in the life of the cotswolds beata moore

F

FRANCES LINCOLN LIMITED
PUBLISHERS

a year in the life of
the cotswolds
beata moore

For John

I would like to express my thanks to John Nicoll for commissioning this book, Nicki Davis and Maria Charalambous respectively for all their help and patience in editing and designing the book, Edward Peake from Sezincote House and Garden, Julie Philips from Rollright Trust Ltd, Alexander Madden from St Michael and All Angels Church in Great Tew, Richard Coombs, Vicar of Swinbrook, Paul Thompson from Manor House Hotel in Castle Combe, Paul Moir from Painswick Rococo Garden, Mike Stripe from the Vintage Sports-Car Club and Blenheim Palace management for their kind permission to take photographs in all the above properties. I would also like to thank my friends Frank and Anne for the very first inspirational trip to the Cotswolds and all other individuals and organisations that helped me while I worked on this book. Finally, I would like to say that this book would not have been created without the help of my husband, John, who has been such a brilliant guide and companion on our frequent trips to the Cotswolds.

Frances Lincoln Limited
4 Torriano Mews
Torriano Avenue
London NW5 2RZ
www.franceslincoln.com

A Year in the Life of the Cotswolds
Copyright © Frances Lincoln Limited 2009

Text and photographs copyright © Beata Moore 2009

First Frances Lincoln edition 2009

A catalogue record for this book is available from the British Library

ISBN 978-0-7112-2859-7

Printed in Singapore

HALF TITLE PAGE Arlington Row in Bibury
TITLE PAGE River Windrush

contents

BIRMINGHAM

Warwick

Worcester

Stratford upon Avon

Banbury

Evesham

Chipping Campden

Blockley

Broadway

Batsford

Tewkesbury

Stanway

Snowshill Hill

Sezincote

Moreton-in-Marsh

Swerford

Winchcombe

Temple Guiting

Rollright Stones

Odda's Chapel

Stow-on-the-Wold

Deerhurst

Chastleton

Great Tew

Chipping Norton

Sudeley

Guiting Power

Condicote

Charlbury

Naunton

The Slaughters

Gloucester

Cheltenham

Leckhampton

Bourton-on-the water

Blenheim Woodstock

Northleach

Lower Chedworth

Burford

Sinbrook

Minster Lovell

Painswick

Coln St Dennis

Bibury

Eastleach

Witney

Oxford

Stroud

Duntisbourne Abbots

Arlington

Quenington

Fairford

Bisley

Cirencester

Uley

Minchinhampton

Owlpen

Nailsworth

Lechlade-on-Thames

Abingdon

Tetbury

Didcot

Malmesbury

Chipping Sodbury

Swindon

Castle Combe

BRISTOL

Chippenham

Lacock

Bath

River Severn

©Maps in Minutes ™/Collins Bartholomew 2007

introduction

Chipping Campden

Set in the heart of the English countryside, the Cotswolds occupies an area of 790 square miles between Gloucester, Bath, Oxford and Stratford-upon-Avon. The Cotswolds is a perfect blend of gentle rolling hills and charming villages built from local honey-coloured limestone. In recognition of the beauty of this quintessentially English countryside, the Cotswolds was designated an Area of Outstanding Natural Beauty in 1966.

The Cotswolds was formed in the Jurassic period of the Mesozoic era, some 150 million years ago. Cotswold hills produce some of the most beautiful and durable limestone to be found anywhere in the world. Limestone is a sedimentary rock formed over millions of years from shells and organisms evolving in warm, shallow sea water. The steep Cotswolds scarp running from Bath to Edge Hill is made up of belts of oolitic limestone. Limestone in the Cotswolds is close enough to the surface of the earth to be easily quarried. This has resulted in its use locally over the centuries as building stone in the construction of almost every building in the region, from simple stone cottages and field boundaries to manor houses, churches and castles. Its golden shade gives the region its distinctive character. The two most characteristic features of Cotswold buildings are a solid foundation and a steep-pitched

roof, necessary for the heavyweight slates and to prevent the rain from penetrating the porous limestone. Quarries were in operation all over the Cotswolds, and today many sites continue extracting and working the stone for repairs and the construction of new buildings.

There have been settlements in the Cotswolds since prehistoric times. Remains from the Neolithic period include long barrows; two of the largest and best preserved of these burial tombs are Belas Knap near Winchcombe and Hetty Pegler's Tump. The famous circle of the Rollright Stones was built approximately 4,500 years ago during the Stone Age. There are remains of hill forts and camps from the Iron Age at Uley Bury, Crickley Hill, Little Sodbury and Painswick Beacon.

Celtic tribes invaded Britain around 500 BC, and the Dabunni tribe built many fortifications along the high points of the Cotswold Edge, establishing Cirencester as their capital. The vast expanse of the Cotswolds was heavily farmed by both Celts and later, the Romans, who brought wealth and prosperity to the area. There are extensive remains of Roman villas at Chedworth and North Leigh with well-preserved mosaics as well as a range of everyday objects. Some of the roads created during the Roman invasion form the basis of today's major routes.

Farmland near Snowshill

OPPOSITE **Sheep at Broadway Hill**

RIGHT **The River Windrush**

BELOW **A disused quarry near Condicote**

The Saxons came from Denmark and Germany in the sixth century and left traces of their culture on the Cotswold landscape. Odda's Chapel in Deerhurst and St Laurence Chapel in Bradford-on-Avon are examples of pure Saxon chapels, and there are several more chapels and churches that stem from Saxon buildings.

Subsequent to William the Conqueror and the Norman Conquest in 1066, the Cotswolds grew in importance as a wool producer. The sheep grazed here had an extremely long fleece and became known as Cotswold lions. The top quality wool produced was in demand across the whole of Europe. The Cotswolds was an ideal place for the wool industry to flourish, not only because of the abundance of sheep but also due to the plentiful supply of water from the Rivers Avon, Windrush and Leach. Water was necessary for cleaning and dyeing the wool and for powering the mills. As a result of the growing demand for wool, towns such as Chipping Campden, Tetbury, Bourton-on-the-Water, Stow-on-the-Wold, Moreton-in-Marsh and Stroud grew and prospered. Medieval churches built in this area by wealthy wool merchants (hence the name wool churches) are examples of some of the finest churches in England.

The Cotswold wool industry went into rapid decline in the nineteenth century, triggered by industrialization and the shift of the wool industry to the north of England. Inevitably, this resulted in a period of economic hardship in the area. In the late nineteenth and early twentieth century, the Arts and Crafts Movement refocused attention on the Cotswolds. William Morris, who co-founded the Pre-Raphaelite Brotherhood and later the famous Morris & Co., rented the Elizabethan Kelmscott Manor in 1871. Craftsmen and artists followed his lead and migrated to the Cotswolds. Morris & Co. produced decorative textiles, wallpapers, furniture, carpets and ceramics and examples of these can be found throughout the Cotswolds.

The Cotswolds of the twenty-first century is a perfect blend of history and beauty and, despite its popularity with tourists, remains tranquil and serene. Picture-perfect, traditional Cotswold villages offer historic sites, friendly pubs and craft shops. Most of the villages and smaller towns have survived unspoilt, and the area boasts many attractions: Corinium Museum in Cirencester; Cotswolds Museum in Bourton-on-the-Water; Gloucester Cathedral; the Roman baths at Bath; Sudeley Castle; Blenheim Palace; and fabulous gardens at Westonbirt, Painswick, Batsford and Hidcote. The countryside, with its gentle hills and open spaces, is ideal for a variety of outdoor activities such as horse riding, cycling, ballooning and walking. All this combines to make the Cotswolds a dream place to live and visit.

LEFT **An Alfa Romeo at Prescott Speed Hill Climb Club**

BELOW **Ballooning in Cirencester**

Fishing in Blenheim Lake

winter

the east

the east

The eastern region of the Cotswolds covers parts of West Oxfordshire with the towns and villages of Chipping Norton, Swerford, Burford, Witney, Woodstock and many more.

Chipping Norton is the highest town in Oxfordshire. It is situated on the slopes of a hillside that was once the site of a Norman castle. Unfortunately, only the earthworks of the castle remain today. 'Chipping' means market, and points to the town's importance as a commercial centre in its early days. Since the thirteenth century people have come to the famous Chipping Norton markets and fairs. Many eighteenth century Georgian houses can be found around the market, while earlier styles remain on New Street. Just outside the town is the impressive Bliss Tweed Mill with its characteristic chimney,

ABOVE **Bliss Mill in Chipping Norton**

LEFT **Whispering Knights megalith monument** (by kind permission of the Rollright Trust Ltd)

visible for miles. It was designed by George Woodhouse in 1872 for local industrialist William Bliss, in a style more suited to a palace than a tweed factory. It contained a glove making factory, a brewery, a tannery and an iron foundry.

Situated in the village of Little Rollright is the mysterious complex of megalith monuments, the **Rollright Stones**. The site consists of three separate elements: the single 2.5-metre high King Stone; a cluster of four standing stones called the Whispering Knights; and a stone circle known as the King's Men. All were built in prehistoric times. The earliest of them, the Whispering Knights, dates from around 4000 BC and was the burial chamber of a portal dolmen where human remains were buried. The King's Men, a ceremonial stone circle, dates from around 2500 BC. The weathered King Stone, possibly marking the site of a Bronze Age cemetery, dates from around 1500 BC. There are many legends and folktales associated with the stones, the most popular about a Danish king and his army who were turned into stones by a witch. All three sites have a long history of witchcraft activities and even today modern neo-pagans and white witches meet here to perform rituals.

Just over 5 miles east of Chipping Norton is the pretty village of **Great Tew**, which dates from around the year 1036. The rustic, thatched-roofed cottages date back to the seventeenth century. Situated on the outskirts of the village is the church of St Michael and All Saints with a decorative Norman south door and beautiful, clearly visible thirteenth century wall paintings.

LEFT Charlbury Fountain commemorates the visit of Queen Victoria in 1886

BELOW Sculptures on the clock tower of St Mary's Church in Fairford

Charlbury, an idyllic little town on the edge of the Wychwood Forest, was originally a Saxon settlement. The town prospered during the eighteenth century thanks to its glove making industry. The town is home to Methodist and Baptist chapels, a Roman Catholic church and St Mary the Virgin Parish Church. Charlbury Museum next to the market house has an interesting collection of artefacts connected with the traditional crafts and industries of the surrounding area. On the outskirts of the town is Lee Place, the former Dower House of Ditchley, at one time visited frequently by Winston Churchill, and now the summer home of the Duke of Marlborough.

The name of the town of **Fairford** originates from the Saxon meaning 'easy ford'. Originally a river-crossing settlement on the River Coln, the heyday of this wool trading town, like many in the Cotswolds, was in the late Middle Ages.

Elegant seventeenth and eighteenth-century houses line the main street, and the Bull Hotel is a former sixteenth-century coaching inn. The oldest part of this lovely town is close to the church of St Mary, a wool church. The elaborate carving on the tower and fascinating grotesques and gargoyles around the parapets are evidence of the prosperity of the area at the time. The church is famed for its twenty-eight magnificent fifteenth-century, pre-Reformation stained glass windows. They form the only complete set of medieval stained glass in the country.

Lechlade-on-Thames is a delightful market town dating back to the early thirteenth century. It nestles on the banks of the River Thames at its highest navigable point. Although it played a part in the Cotswolds wool trade, it was mainly a staging post for goods and passenger traffic. The centre of the town has a number of interesting old buildings and shops as

BELOW **Church of St Lawrence in Lechlade-on-Thames**

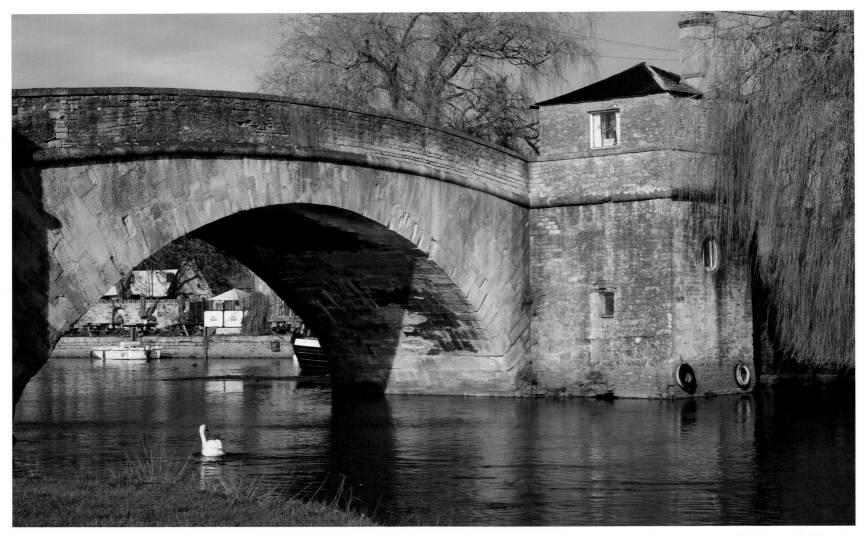

well as the church of St Lawrence that was completed in 1476. The slender spire of this wool church is a landmark visible for miles. A short walk from the town, St John's Lock, the highest lock on the Thames, can be found. Guarding the lock is the Neptune-like statue of *Old Father Thames* by Rafaelle Monti. Today, recreation and leisure boats have replaced trading on this wide and slow moving part of the river.

Two sleepy villages, **Eastleach Turville** and **Eastleach Martin** sit astride the River Leach. The clapper bridge crossing the Leach connecting the villages is called Keble's Bridge in honour of John Keble, a popular Victorian curate, founding member of the Oxford Movement and author of many popular hymns. St Andrew's Church in Eastleach Turville is of Norman origin, with decorative Norman carving above the south door. It faces the church of St Michael and St Martin in the parish of Eastleach Martin, which was much restored in the Victorian era.

The town of **Burford** on the River Windrush was the site of a fortified ford in Anglo-Saxon times. It is now dominated by a steep high street, lined with seventeenth and eighteenth-century golden Cotswold stone Tudor and Georgian buildings. Most of the shops lining the street are shallow and single storey with workshops behind and living quarters on the upper floors. The fifteenth-century parish church of St John the Baptist,

originally Norman, was remodelled in the fifteenth century. The restoration of the church included scraping off the medieval plaster, prompting William Morris to found the Society for the Preservation of Ancient Buildings. 'This church, sir, is mine, and if I choose to, I shall stand on my head in it,' was the response of the local vicar to criticism from Morris.

The architecture of the small village of **Swinbrook** is typically Cotswolds. The small parish church of St Mary houses the Fettiplace monuments, a striking pair of seventeenth-century family tombs. They are most unusual, but a fitting memorial to one of the biggest landowning families in Oxfordshire. Beyond the church is the grave of the novelist Nancy Mitford, author of *Love in a Cold Climate*, and her famous socialite sisters known for their Fascist sympathies; Unity Mitford, Diana Mosley and Pamela Mitford. Their Elizabethan manor is nearby, in Asthall.

The village of **Minster Lovell** is one of the loveliest villages in the Windrush valley. It has a 500-year-old bridge spanning the River Windrush, rows of elegant stone buildings and perhaps the most important romantic ruin of the fifteenth century: Minster Lovell Hall. This spectacular place was built on the banks of the River Windrush in 1440 for Lord William Lovell. Sadly, the magnificent building was dismantled in 1747 and today only the ruins of the great hall, the entrance porch

ABOVE **Halfpenny bridge in Lechlade-on-Thames**

BELOW *Old Father Thames* **by Rafaelle Monti, St John's Lock in Lechlade-on-Thames**

LEFT **The Leach River in Eastleach Martin**

BELOW **Eastleach Turville**

BELOW **Norman carving
above the south door of
St Andrew's Church,
Eastleach Turville**

BOTTOM **Snowdrops,
St Andrew's Church,
Eastleach Turville**

and one of the towers survive. A grim tale is associated with the hall: Francis, the last Baron Lovell, disappeared shortly after the Lambert Simnel rebellion. In 1708 a secret underground room was found, together with what was said to be the skeleton of Francis Lovell sitting at a table. The story goes that to avoid persecution Lovell hid in this safe place, but when his trusty servant died suddenly, he was unable to get out and died a terrible death of starvation.

The village of **Woodstock**, 10 miles north of Oxford, was founded in 1163. Woodstock means 'settlement in the woods' and true to its name, the original settlement was in the middle of a forest reserved for the King's hunting. Although Woodstock is famous for its proximity to Blenheim Palace, the beauty of the old town and the inviting pubs and restaurants helped to seal its fame as one of the most charming towns in the Oxfordshire Cotswolds. There are some very interesting buildings here: the Bear Inn which dates from the thirteenth century; the sixteenth-century merchant's house now home to the Oxfordshire County Museum; the eighteenth-century Town Hall; the church of St Mary Magdalene from the twelfth century; and the nearby parish church of St Martin in Bladon, the burial site of Sir Winston Churchill.

Blenheim Palace is the ancestral home of the Churchill family. Here, Britain's great Prime Minister, Sir Winston Churchill, was born in 1874. This grand palace set in 2,100 acres of parkland is a World Heritage Site. In the twelfth century, Henry I built a deer park and hunting lodge here. Henry II was a frequent visitor when he entertained his famous mistress 'Fair Rosamund', the daughter of Walter de Clifford. Woodstock Manor was where Princess Elizabeth was imprisoned by Queen Mary. The manor subsequently became Blenheim Palace, built between 1705 and 1724 by John Vanbrugh for John Churchill, 1st Duke of Marlborough. This grand building was a gift from a grateful nation as a reward for the victory over the French at the Battle of Blenheim. The palace houses a collection of unique wall tapestries, paintings, furniture and other fine decorative objects. The garden and the park were landscaped by celebrated eighteenth-century landscape gardener Lancelot 'Capability' Brown. He surpassed all expectations in creating the exquisite gardens with breathtaking vistas.

ABOVE The church of St
John the Baptist, Burford

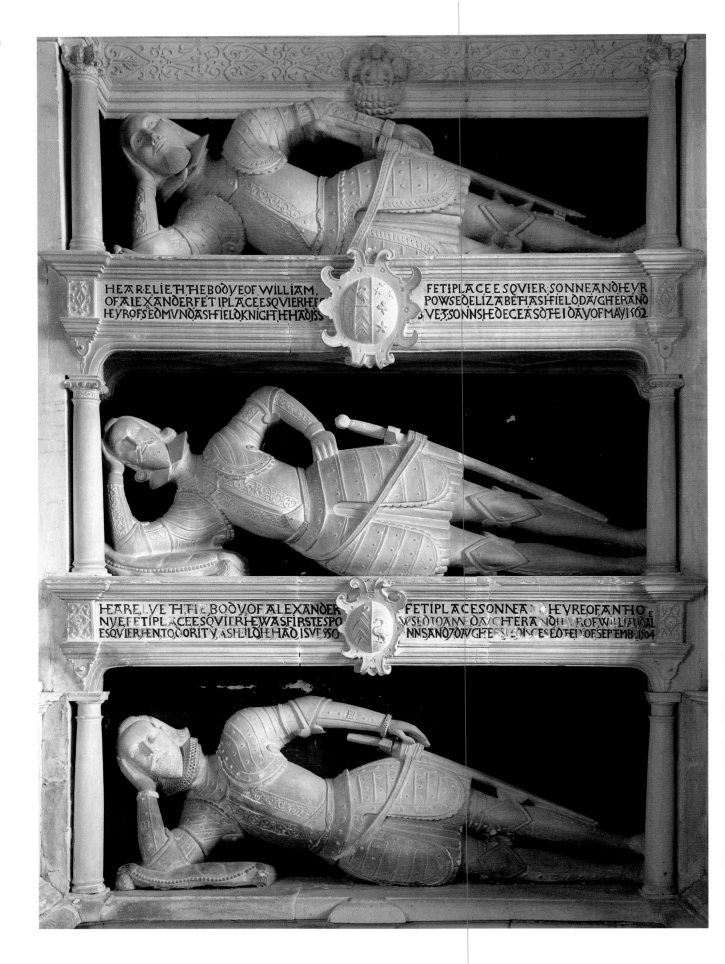

Swinbrook village

Dovecote, Minster Lovell

The church of St Kenelm
and ruins of Minster
Lovell Hall

RIGHT **Entrance to Blenheim Park**

BELOW **Sir John Vanbrugh's Grand Bridge in the grounds of Blenheim Palace**

The water terraces, Blenheim

LEFT The water terraces, Blenheim

TOP The cascade at Blenheim

ABOVE Angelic statue in the formal garden
of Blenheim

The mermaid fountain
by Waldo Story in
the Italian garden
of Blenheim

spring

the south

the south

The southern part of the Cotswolds stretches south of Gloucestershire including the towns and villages of Bibury, Northleach, Painswick, Bisley, Tetbury and Cirencester.

Bibury quite justifiably earned from William Morris the title of most beautiful village in England. The village is a conservation area and is home to the picturesque weavers' cottages of Arlington Row. The honey-coloured stone cottages with steeply pitched roofs were built in 1380 and converted into cottages in the seventeenth century. Nestled next to a gentle stream with a footbridge, they are the subject of many a photograph. Nearby, the Arlington Mill with its working water wheel houses a folk and agricultural museum. St Mary's Church dates from the eighth century, but Norman and Gothic additions are also visible.

Northleach is a town on the Roman Fosse Way. The town centre is surrounded by rows of medieval cottages, and many of the fifteenth and sixteenth-century merchants' houses are half-timbered. The eighteenth-century old prison, better known as the House of Correction, is now a museum of rural life. The local fifteenth-century church of St Peter and St Paul is a grand example of Perpendicular architecture, and is often referred to as the Cathedral of the Cotswolds. Close to Northleach stands Chedworth Roman Villa, one of the largest Romano-British villas in the country.

The charming village of **Painswick** is often called the queen of the Cotswolds. New Street, built in the early fifteenth century, has the oldest building in England to house a post office, and

Bibury Bridge over the River Coln

the Falcon Hotel has the oldest bowling green in the country. Two fourteenth-century houses on Bisley Street, the Chur and Byfield House, still have original donkey doors wide enough for donkeys carrying wool from the local mills. Most of the elegant church of St Mary dates from the fifteenth and sixteenth centuries. The graveyard has many unusual seventeenth-century raised pedestal tombs and a long avenue of ornamental clipped yew trees. According to legend the total number of trees would never exceed ninety-nine, and should another tree grow the devil would pull it out. The village is well known for the delightful Rococo Garden, originally laid out in the eighteenth century in a 6-acre valley. Over the years the garden fell into neglect but restoration in the 1980s resulted in the recreation of this unique and beautiful garden.

Nestled high in the hills in the heart of the Cotswolds is the village of **Bisley**. It stands over 700 feet above sea level and overlooks the Frome Valley. Bisley is very charming with wonderful winding streets and buildings rising in terraces. The local legend of the Bisley Boy claims that Princess Elizabeth, future Queen Elizabeth I, died unexpectedly during her stay at the Manor of Bisley. When King Henry VIII sent for her, her minders, panicked and fearful, decided to replace her with another child. They had no success finding a red headed young girl, and so, the story goes, replaced her with a boy, the illegitimate son of Henry VIII and Elizabeth Blunt. The substitution was never discovered.

Monet style footbridge in Bibury

LEFT Garden decoration in the Rococo Gardens at Painswick

BELOW LEFT Painswick Rococo Gardens

BELOW RIGHT Pedestal tombs at St Mary's Church in Painswick

Duntisbourne Abbots is a picturesque village with pretty narrow lanes lined with seventeenth-century cottages. St Peter's Church dates from the twelfth century, built on a Saxon church site. The Norman tower has interesting belfry lights of pierced stone lattice-work and inside the church there is an early thirteenth-century font. Nearby the village a hoar stone stands at the entrance to a Neolithic long barrow. According to local legend, at midnight the stones surrounding the long barrow begin running round the field, which explains the name, the Devil's flights, given to the field.

Minchinhampton is situated high on the Cotswold Edge, above the town of Stroud. Minchinhampton is a very attractive town with many fine buildings dating from the seventeenth and eighteenth centuries. As with many Cotswolds towns the wool industry brought wealth to the area. The imposing columned market house, built in 1698, is situated close to the market cross, and is a good spot to get a view of the town. Minchinhampton Common to the north of the town offers great views of the surrounding countryside with some interesting long barrows and mounds from the Iron Age.

Owlpen Manor is steeped in 900 years of history. The imposing grey limestone manor is of mixed architectural style and is surrounded by terraced gardens. The house is said to be haunted by Margaret of Anjou, Queen consort of Henry VI. She stayed at Owlpen on the second night of May, before the 1471 Battle of Tewkesbury, one of the decisive battles during the War of the Roses, where her husband and only son, Prince Edward, were murdered. Wearing a fur-trimmed gown, steeple hat and wimple, it is claimed she drifts through the rooms on the eve of the battle.

The town of **Tetbury**, on the route from Oxford to Bristol, was once a thriving wool market town. The central part of the town is largely unchanged, with many seventeenth and eighteenth-century wool merchants' houses. The market, designed for the sale of wool and yarn, is supported by three rows of solid stone pillars. The Chipping Steps lead to a steep street with medieval stone cottages and to the famous Gumstool Hill, the site of the annual woolsack races. Each year this impressive event, first held in the seventeenth century, sees competitors race up and down the steep hill with 60 lb woolsacks.

Malmesbury is positioned at the southern fringe of the Cotswolds near the River Avon. This attractive little town, often called the queen of hilltop towns, flourished in the Middle Ages as a weaving and silk centre. It is home to many interesting almshouses, taverns, mills, lock-ups and picturesque bridges, but is most famous for its imposing Norman abbey. Today, the existing part of the abbey is only a third of the size of the original. This impressive building dates back to the twelfth century, although an earlier monastery was established here in the year 676. In the fifteenth century, the towers of the abbey collapsed, causing substantial damage to the rest of the building. Left neglected for centuries, it was only in the twentieth century that restoration work began. Malmesbury Abbey is also the site of an early attempt at flight by the eccentric monk Eilmer, who, in the year 1010, constructed a pair of wings and launched himself from the tower. Unfortunately for him, he glided for only 200 yards before landing heavily, breaking both of his legs.

Lying in the lush valley by the banks of the River Bybrook, Castle Combe is one of the prettiest villages in England.

The heart of the village is at the crossing of the main streets, near the fourteenth-century market cross. Next to it are the remains of the Butter Cross, marking the site of the fifteenth-century market hall. St Andrew's Church, thought to date from the twelfth century, was restored in the nineteenth century. Perhaps the most interesting features of the church are the parapet with fifty beautifully carved stone heads, and the tomb of Walter de Dunstanville, whose family owned the castle. The site of the original castle is half a mile north west of the manor house, but hardly any traces of the castle remain, just some earthworks. The fourteenth-century manor house has over the years been altered and enlarged and eventually turned into a luxury hotel. The end of this remarkable village is marked with a stone bridge guarded, according to romantic local legend, by the ghost of a Roman soldier.

Cirencester, a historically important Roman town, lies on the River Churn, a tributary of the River Thames. It can justifiably lay claim to the title the capital of the Cotswolds. The town was built after the invasion led by Emperor Claudius in AD 43 and named Corinium Dobunnorum. Very quickly it became the regional capital of Roman Britain, second only to London. Most of the present town of Cirencester dates from the Middle Ages. The famous St Mary's Abbey situated behind the market place was consecrated in 1176. Unfortunately during the dissolution it was almost completely demolished. Nearby Cirencester House is the family seat of the Earl of Bathurst. The spectacular Cirencester Park is a fine example of baroque geometric design. The parish church of St John the Baptist dominates the centre of the town, the largest parish church in Gloucestershire. The famous Corinium Museum traces the history of the area from the Iron Age, with emphasis on the Romano-British era. To the south of the city, on Cotswold Avenue, there is one of the largest Roman amphitheatres in Britain, built in the early second century.

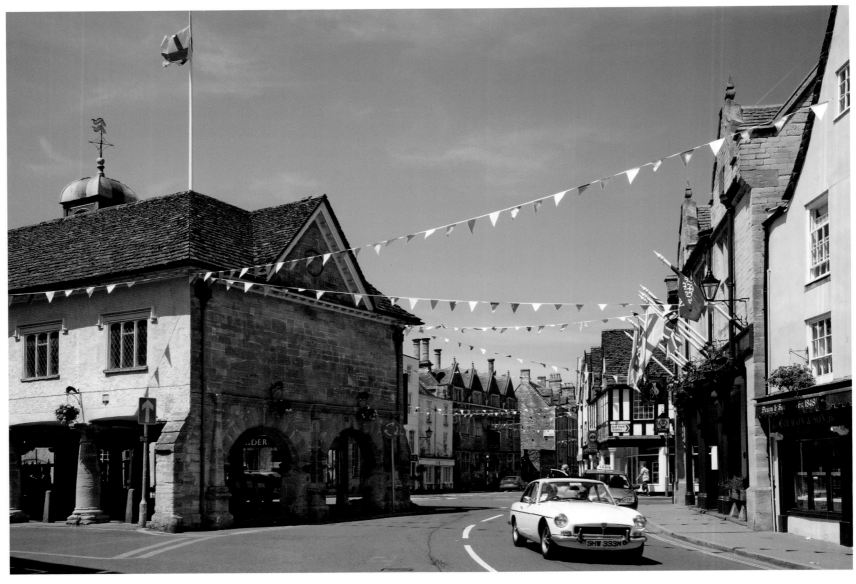

BELOW **Tetbury market house**

ABOVE **Malmesbury Abbey**

RIGHT **The Birdcage,**
Malmesbury's fifteenth-century
market cross.

The city of **Bath**, with its riches of Roman, medieval and Georgian architecture is a designated World Heritage Site. First dwellings were built around three natural hot mineral springs. Romans built the temple to the Sulis Minerva in AD 60 to 70 as well as the extensive thermal spa. Medieval times brought prosperity generated from the wool industry, but it was only in the eighteenth century that the city began its rapid development. At this time it was transformed into a fashionable health resort and gained its classical architecture thanks to a charismatic socialite Richard 'Beau' Nash, entrepreneur Ralph Allen and talented architects John Wood the Elder and his son, John Wood the Younger. The world famous ancient baths boast some of the finest Roman remains in Europe. They were built some two thousand years ago, forgotten for centuries and unearthed again in the Victorian era. Next to the baths is the famous Georgian Pump Room. This elegant neo-classical building was the social heart of Bath for centuries. At present a restaurant, it still offers the special mineral water to visitors. Bath Abbey, standing in the heart of the city, was founded in 1499 and is a beautiful example of Perpendicular Gothic architecture. The abbey's most interesting features are the fan vaulting, flying buttresses, imaginative carving of Prior Birde's chantry, castellated pierced parapet and stained glass windows. In the west font two Jacobs' ladders carved in stone stretch from heaven to earth, with carved figures of angels ascending. The Royal Crescent was built by John Wood the Younger between 1767 and 1775. His masterpiece is one of the finest crescents in Europe; it forms a semi-ellipse of thirty elegant Grade I listed mansions. The façade is decorated by 114 giant order Ionic columns. Pulteney Bridge unites east and west Bath over the River Avon. The bridge designed by Robert Adam in 1771 is based on the Ponte Vecchio in Florence. It consists of three lofty arches and is one of only four bridges in all of Europe that contains shops.

Market square and parish
church of St John the
Baptist in Cirencester

LEFT AND ABOVE **Royal Crescent, Bath**

ABOVE **The King's and Queen's Baths**

summer

the north

the north

The northern Cotswolds covers the northern part of Gloucestershire and includes the towns and villages of Winchcombe, Snowshill, Broadway, Chipping Campden, Moreton-in-Marsh and many more.

Winchcombe, an attractive market town, was the ancient Saxon capital of Mercia. St Peter's Parish Church is renowned for the forty grotesque gargoyles which date from 1468. It has been suggested that each figure represented a local character from the time. Years later, one of the figures was the model for Lewis Carroll's Mad Hatter. On the outskirts of Winchcombe is the spectacular medieval Sudeley Castle, with an abundance of towers, turrets and terraces. Katharine Parr, Henry VIII's sixth wife, lived at Sudeley Castle and is buried in the chapel. The

ruins of Hailes Abbey, founded in 1246, are less than a mile away from Winchcombe.

Nearby Hailes Abbey is a magnificent Cotswold stone manor house, **Stanway House**. Started in Elizabethan times and completed in the Jacobean period, it has hardly been altered over the centuries. It has a jewel-like gatehouse, towering multi-paned windows in the grand hall and elaborate furniture within the house. The extensive grounds include the tithe barn, pond, cascade, pyramid and a single-jet 300-foot fountain in the canal, the world's tallest gravity fountain.

The village of **Snowshill** above Buckland and Laverton is surrounded by lavendar fields. Perfectly straight lines of vivid purple plants provide a beautiful view associated more with

Provence than with the heart of the Cotswolds. Snowshill is the home of Snowshill Manor which was originally owned by Winchcombe Abbey, but after the dissolution of the monasteries was given by Henry VIII to Katherine Parr. Over the years it changed hands many times. In 1919 it was bought by Charles Paget Wade who quickly filled the manor with various artifacts including toys, armour, furniture, bicycles, tapestries and musical instruments.

Broadway village is known as the northern gateway to the Cotswolds. It is renowned for its mix of Tudor, Georgian and Stuart styles of architecture. Originally a stage coach stop on the Worcester to London coaching route, it was home to some two dozens inns. At the heart of the village is the Lygon Arms Hotel known for hosting Oliver Cromwell and Charles I. The main street is lined with red chestnut trees and there are plenty of craft boutiques, fine antique shops and restaurants. At the top of the escarpment is Broadway Tower, built by the Earl of Coventry in 1798. Broadway Hill and Tower offer spectacular views over as many as thirteen counties. It was a favourite retreat for William Morris and his friends.

Chipping Campden, frequently described as the jewel in the crown of the Cotswolds, is one of the most charming towns in the area. It was established in the fourteenth century as a busy wool traders' town. The main street is flanked by buildings of varying architectural style. At the centre of the town stands the impressive Jacobean market hall of 1627. The medieval church of St James was completed in 1500 and its 120-foot pinnacle tower is a landmark visible for miles around. Next to the church there is the gateway to the old seventeenth-century Campden House, which unfortunately burnt down during the Civil War. Close to the church is a row of beautiful 1612 almshouses. Since 1610 the town has been home to the peculiar Cotswold Olimpicks. They are held every summer on Dover's Hill and include such bizarre games as shin-kicking, single stick fighting, and climbing the unclimbable ladder, among others.

The village of **Blockley** lies in a pleasant valley, alongside a picturesque winding brook. Blockley thrived in the eighteenth and nineteenth centuries when the village was the main centre of the silk industry. The brook used to provide power for twelve silk mills, Westmacott Mill the largest of them. The village green overlooks the popular bowling green and beautiful Norman church of St Peter and St Paul.

Created as a 'wild' garden in the late 1880s, **Batsford Arboretum**, encompasses 50 acres of land and contains over one thousand five hundred trees. The arboretum was designed and planted by Lord Redesdale. He was influenced deeply by his travels as British Envoy in Japan and China and decided to bring distinctly Japanese elements into this typically English setting. Cotswold Falconry Centre in Batsford Park, with it's large variety of birds of prey, gives a remarkable insight into the ancient art of falconry.

Thoroughly unconventional, **Sezincote House** and its garden is an extraordinary mixture of Indian and English styles. The estate was purchased in 1795 by Colonel John Cockerell, who left it to his youngest brother Charles when he died in 1798. Sir Charles Cockerell, who had made his fortune in India, decided to build his house in the fashionable Mogul style of Rajasthan. The Prince Regent was a visitor to Sezincote and the house is said to be the inspiration for the Royal Pavilion in Brighton. The house is decorated with Indian motifs, turrets and onion dome, while in the garden one can find an Indian bridge with statues of bulls and a temple dedicated to Surya, the Hindu deity of the sun.

ABOVE **Stanway gatehouse**

LEFT **Stanway war memorial**

LEFT The graveyard of the nineteenth-century church of St Barnabas in Snowshill

BELOW Lavender field near Snowshill

Moreton-in-Marsh is one of the bigger market towns in the northern Cotswolds. Situated on the Fosse Way, it dates back a thousand years to the Saxon era. The High Street has many elegant eighteenth-century inns and houses, and in the centre of the town is Redesdale Hall, built in 1887 by the owner of Batsford Park. The town is famous for its excellent hotels and restaurants but is also renowned for a number of ghosts. The Manor House Hotel is supposedly haunted by Dame Creswycke, the Redesdale Arms Hotel by a very noisy ghost, and the Fire Service College, on the grounds of an old airfield, by the ghost of an aeroplane from the Second World War.

Near to Moreton-in-Marsh is the village of **Chastleton** with the historic Chastleton House. It is one of the finest and most complete Jacobean houses to be found in England, proudly standing next to the twelfth-century village church. Chastleton House was completed in 1612 for William Jones, a wealthy wool merchant. The house is filled with interesting everyday objects, rare tapestries, portraits, furniture and textiles, while outside there is a classic Elizabethan topiary garden and England's first croquet lawn. It was here that the rules of this quintessentially English game were drawn up in 1865.

At nearly 800 feet, **Stow-on-the-Wold** is the highest town in the Cotswolds. It sits at an intersection of seven major roads, including the Roman Fosse Way. Like many old Cotswold towns, Stow's prosperity grew as a market town involved with the sheep trade. Even today, the market place is the centre of activity and is surrounded by pubs, antique and souvenir shops. On Digbeth Street stands the Royalist Hotel, believed to be the oldest coach inn in England, dating back to AD 947. The church of St Edward that overlooks the market square was built between the eleventh and fifteenth centuries.

Bourton-on-the-Water, one of the prettiest villages in the Cotswolds, is often referred to as the Venice of the Cotswolds or little Venice. The Windrush River enters the village over the rapids next to the Old Mill and flows under elegant low stone bridges. The earliest stone bridge is Mill Bridge, built in 1654. Many buildings on both sides of the riverbank are over four hundred years old, dating back to Elizabethan times. –St Lawrence Parish Church dates from the fourteenth century, but the only visible part from this era is the chancel, built in 1328 by Walter de Burhton. Bourton-on-the-Water has a number of tourist attractions, including Cotswold Motor Museum, Birdland and the model village.

Close to Bourton-on-the-Water are the villages of **Upper** and **Lower Slaughter**, standing near the River Eye, a tributary of the nearby Windrush. The name Slaughter is derived from the Old English word *slohtre* meaning 'muddy place'. Upper Slaughter lies on a grassy slope above the stream. The village is dominated by the fifteenth-century manor house, now a hotel. St Peter's Parish Church with its many early tombstones dates back to Richard the Lionheart's reign. The village of Lower Slaughter is crossed by two narrow stone footbridges. The old corn mill with its restored water wheel and distinctive red brick tower offers a museum, craft shop and tea room. The seventeenth-century Lower Slaughter Manor stands in its own lovely gardens next to St Mary's Church.

A few miles away from Lower Slaughter, tucked away in the Windrush Valley, is the village of **Naunton**. Its famous gabled fifteenth-century dovecote housed thousands of birds in the past, and is now a grade II listed building. Due to its positioning by the river, it was converted in the eighteenth century to a mill for grinding corn. The local church has a Perpendicular tower with interesting eighteenth-century sundials.

Guiting Power is an attractive village of sturdy Cotswold cottages surrounding a small village green. It is listed in the Domesday survey of 1086 as a royal holding. The village lies on a tributary of the River Windrush. The church of St Michael and All Angels dates from early Norman times and it has an exceptionally fine Norman south doorway. The stone war memorial in the form of a medieval stone cross is the focal point of the village.

Nearby **Temple Guiting** acquired the prefix Temple in the twelfth century, as the manor in the village was owned by the Knights Templar. The local church, St Mary's, contains beautifully carved heads that adorn the corbel table around the exterior of the chancel, wooden panels of the Georgian decalogue of 1748 over the south door and three stained glass panels dating from the late fifteenth century.

ABOVE St James' Church in Chipping Campden

OPPOSITE ABOVE LEFT The market hall in Chipping Campden

OPPOSITE ABOVE RIGHT Chipping Campden High Street

OPPOSITE BOTTOM The gatehouse, the only surviving part of Campden House

FAR LEFT Church of
St Peter and St Paul
in Blockley

LEFT Blockley bowling
green

BELOW Golden eagle
and eagle owl in
the Cotswold Falconry
Centre in Batsford Park

ABOVE Sezincote House

RIGHT Hindu temple
dedicated to the goddess
Surya in Sezincote

TOP LEFT **Redesdale Hall in Moreton-in-Marsh**

TOP RIGHT **Moreton-in-Marsh war memorial**

LEFT **Chastleton House**

RIGHT The north porch of
St Edward's Church in
Stow-on-the-Wold

BELOW Stow-on-the-Wold
market

ABOVE **Bourton-on-the-Water**

OPPOSITE **Cotswold Motor Museum, Bourton-on-the-Water**

Stone bridges in
Bourton-on-the-Water

ABOVE Lower Slaughter
Manor House Hotel

LEFT Clapper bridge
across the River Eye
in Lower Slaughter

Lower Slaughter cottages
and old corn mill

ABOVE A fifteenth-century dovecote in Naunton

LEFT The Black Horse pub in Naunton

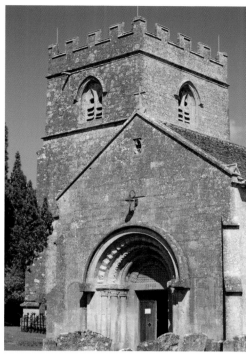

FAR LEFT The war memorial in
Guiting Power

LEFT The church of St Michael
and All Angels in Guiting Power

BELOW Guiting Power

autumn

the west

the west

The western part of the Cotswolds includes the Severn Vale and the Vale of Barkeley with the towns and villages of Cheltenham, Gloucester, Tewkesbury and many more.

    Cheltenham is the most complete Regency town in England. It is situated on the edge of the Cotswold Hills and is known as the gateway to the Cotswolds. Cheltenham began as an Anglo-Saxon settlement and the name of the town is derived from the Saxon *Celtenhomme* meaning 'the town under the hill'. In the Domesday Book of 1086 it is noted as a small village with a population of less than 200. In 1226 it became a market town and by the seventeenth century the population reached approximately 1,500. With the discovery of the natural springs some 300 years ago, it developed into a fashionable health resort. According to local legend, pigeons first made the discovery of the mineral water as they pecked at the salty deposits. People believed that the local waters could heal all manner of illness and the visit of King George II in 1788 sealed the towns popularity. A number of new spas were created, including Montpellier Spa and magnificent gardens started in 1809 and Sherborne Spa in 1818. Cheltenham's heyday lasted from about 1790 to 1840 and the town was visited by many famous people, including Princess Victoria, Lord Byron, Jane

RIGHT Statue of Gustav
Holst, famous composer,
born in Cheltenham

BELOW Pittville Pump
Room in Cheltenham

Austen and the Duke of Wellington. Many fine gardens and Regency buildings were created at this time. Cheltenham's famous promenade dates back to 1818. Neptune's Fountain, beautifully designed by Joseph Hall, was added in 1893 resembling the famous Trevi Fountain in Rome, though on a smaller scale. Stately lime trees border the Montpellier Gardens. Opposite, Montpellier Walk with its elegant shops is famous for the caryatids – more than thirty beautifully carved pillars. Their classical female shape is based on figures from the Acropolis in Athens. The River Chelt runs through Sandford Park, where colourful plants are set around the Unwin Fountain. Perhaps the most famous feature of Cheltenham is Pittville Park, the city's largest ornamental park, built in 1825 with the magnificent colonnaded and domed Pittville Pump Room. Built for elegant balls and entertainment, it is prominently set in the lavish parkland surrounded by a lake, bridges and walkways lined with trees and bushes.

North of Cheltenham, two intriguing Saxon churches can be found in the small village of **Deerhurst**. One of the most complete Saxon chapels in England is Odda's Chapel built in 1056 by Earl Odda, a powerful Saxon noble during the reign of Edward the Confessor. This tiny building is a simple two-cell church composed of a nave and a chapel. Reverend George Butterworth, Vicar of Deerhurst, rediscovered Odda's Chapel in 1885. At present, the chapel is attached to a half-timbered farmhouse. The stone inscription from the chapel reads: 'Earl Odda had this Royal Hall built and dedicated in honour of the Holy Trinity for the soul of his brother, Aelfric, which left the body in this place. Bishop Ealdred dedicated it the second of the Ides of April in the fourteenth year of the reign of Edward, King of the English.' (12th April 1056)

ABOVE Suburbs of
Cheltenham at sunrise

OPPOSITE Morning fog
near Cheltenham

The second fascinating church in Deerhurst is St Mary's Church. It was founded around the year 800 and is almost entirely Saxon, with some later additions. The restoration of the building in the nineteenth century uncovered many interesting Anglo-Saxon features. A short walk to the back of the church leads to a beautiful Saxon angel carving adorning the south side of the ninth-century apse.

Tewkesbury is an attractive historic town at the meeting point of the Rivers Severn and Avon. Tewkesbury is said to be named after a Saxon monk, Theoc, who founded a hermitage here in the seventh century. In the Saxon tongue the town was called Theocsbury. Evidence of not only Saxon but also Roman occupation can be found in archaeological excavations around the town. Over the centuries, Tewkesbury's fortunes, like most of the more prosperous towns in the Cotswolds, depended on the wool and milling industries. Today, one of these mills, Abbey Mill, still stands, though it has been converted for residential use. The medieval layout and character of the town has survived and the many half-timbered Tudor buildings, overhanging upper storeys, carved doorways and fascinating maze of small alleyways make it one of the finest medieval towns in England. Tewkesbury's spectacular abbey was founded by Robert FitzHamon at the end of the eleventh century as a Benedictine monastery but building of the present abbey did not start until 1102. It has numerous important medieval tombs and the central tower, at 148 feet, is the tallest surviving Norman tower in the world. Most of the monastery buildings, as well as the vineyards, were destroyed during the time of the dissolution of the monasteries, but the abbey building was saved by the local people, who bought it for the sum of £453. Tewkesbury has over two hundred listed buildings and was designated a Conservation Area in 1967.

Gloucester, positioned in the lush Severn Valley, is overlooked by the Cotswold Hills. Britain's most inland port has a lively and colourful past, from its Roman foundations to its Victorian docklands. The Roman fortified port was established here at Kingsholm in AD 48 for 5,000 soldiers. The new town was called Glevum and later it received the status of Colonia – the highest urban status in the Empire. Numerous Roman antiquities have been discovered in and around Gloucester.

Sunrise near Cheltenham

+ ODDA DVX IVSSIT hNC
REGIAM AVLAM CONSTRVI
ATQVE DEDICARI IN HONO
RĒ S TRINITATIS PRO ANIMA ER
MANIS VI ÆLFRICI QVE DE HOC
LOCO ASVPTA EALDREDVS VERO
EPS QVI EANDĒ DEDICAVIT III ID
BVS APL X IIII AV ANNOS REG
NI EADWARDI REGIS ANGLORV̄

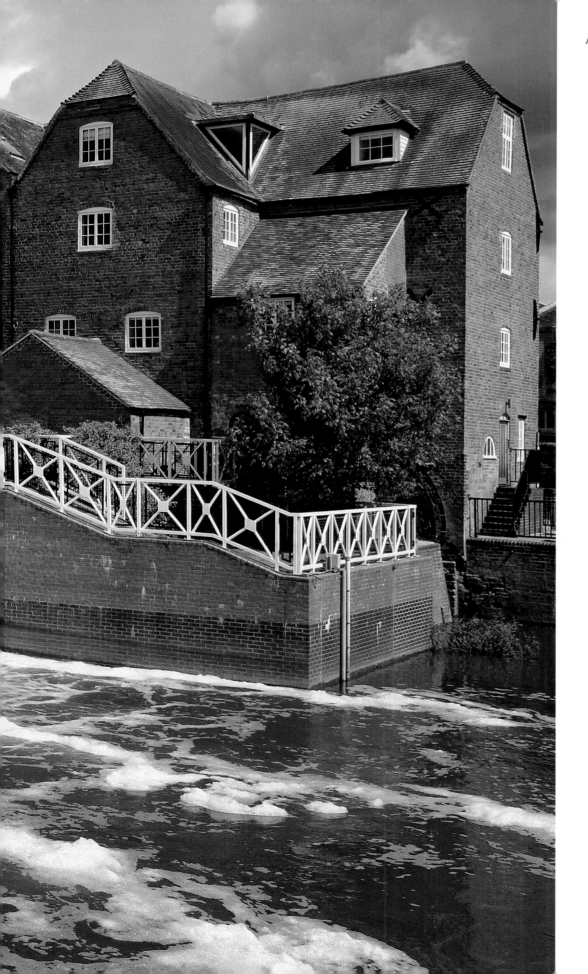

Abbey Mill in Tewkesbury

St Oswald's Anglo-
Saxon minster and
medieval priory

In AD 577, following the battle of Dyrham, the Saxons captured the town. The slow decline of the city under Saxon rule was revived around the year 900. The daughter of Alfred the Great built new fortifications, a royal palace and established the royal chapel of St Oswald. In the centuries that followed, St Oswald's grew in importance due to the many pilgrimages made. In 1153 the church that housed St Oswald's shrine was turned into a priory. Another priory, Llanthony Secunda, was built in 1137 by the displaced monks from Llanthony Priory in Wales. The priory was dissolved in 1538 and only a small part of it remained in use by the parish church. Today, what is left of the old priory is protected as a Scheduled Ancient Monument. In the Middle Ages, Gloucester became a significant port and the market town for the surrounding region. Its main industry was wool and leather. In 1541 Gloucester was given a bishop and the abbey church was made the new cathedral. Despite being a port since Roman times, it was only in 1580 that Gloucester was granted the full and official status of port by Queen Elizabeth I. Although Gloucester's docks are further from the sea than any other in Britain, they were busy with tall ocean-going ships from all over the world. The establishment of the artificial docks and canals in the Victorian period transformed Gloucester into a successful and important centre for the shipment of timber, coal, stone and foodstuffs. Many of the historic warehouses today have been restored and converted to museums, shops, restaurants and flats.

OPPOSITE **Statue on the south porch of Gloucester Cathedral**

RIGHT Baker's shop in
Gloucester

BELOW Folk Museum,
Gloucester

ABOVE **Historic docks,
Gloucester**

Gloucester Cathedral, originally an Anglo-Saxon monastery, became a Benedictine abbey in 1027 and was rebuilt between 1047 and 1062. The cathedral has a combination of Gothic, Anglo-Norman and Romanesque architecture and is regarded as one of the most beautiful architectural gems in Britain. Nearby, the Blackfriars original medieval cloister, completed in 1239, is believed to be England's oldest surviving library building. It was used as a library and scriptorium for monks copying the Bible. After the priory was dissolved all surviving buildings were bought by a prosperous cloth maker, Thomas Bell. It remained in private hands until the twentieth century. The surviving parts of Greyfriars Monastery, founded by Thomas, Lord of Berkeley Castle, were incorporated into a Georgian building which now houses Gloucester Music Library. The Folk Museum, housed in three Tudor and Jacobean timber framed buildings (the so-called Bishop Hooper's lodgings), is one of Britain's oldest museums dedicated to social history. The House of the Tailor of Gloucester at 9 College Court, in the alley leading to Gloucester Cathedral, is a wonderful little museum and a shop selling Beatrix Potter memorabilia.

index